Understanding Programming

Languages

Aditya Yadav

Copyright

Understanding Programming Languages

Copyright © 2009 by Aditya Yadav

ISBN-13: 978-1-451-53116-9

To Baby Alisha Who Has Made Me Realize

How Beautiful Life Can Be

Contents

Foreword

Over the years I have worked with organizations who were never on the cutting edge of technology. The reasons for which were partly the risk involved, partly the knowledge and biases of their leading practitioners, the ambiguity around programming languages as they evolve, lack of time to follow each development, and lack of a guide they could use to quickly compare programming languages, evaluate, make decisions and adopt them. This book has been an attempt to answer a lot of how's and why's around programming languages in general.

During my stint at my p2p startup I realized that being on this side technologists think mostly in terms of breakthroughs while businesses on the other side think mostly in terms of how it solves their problems and issues. Business doesn't typically care about which language the solution is implemented in, they have other issues around maintainability and risk. I have been told by CXO's of some of the biggest companies in the world, companies that have all the money to hire the best people, that they don't have the people with PolyGlot skills. They usually have roles like Java Developer, C# Developer, VB.Net developer, Scala Developer, PL/SQL Developer and so on. And every region their office is in has its own preferences of languages. They try to attack the problem by creating an approved stack of technologies and languages. Which works to an extent but doesn't solve the problem.

The problem still remains that the world has changed drastically in the last couple of years and language mashups are a reality. On the other hand even if one language is to be chosen for a project usually the choices are between C# and

Java. There are a multitude of languages to choose from. How do we understand which ones are good for what and how do we compare them?

This book is not specific to any one particular language. It covers the basic design elements of languages. I would say that this book is for the technically inclined but the subject of this book is as much a subject for a leaders/managers purview as it is for developers and architects.

This book doesn't contain any opinions about merits of one language over another. It just stops at presenting the criteria to make comparisons. An actual comparison could change over time as languages evolve and we will refrain from making hard statements. It is left to the reader to gain an understanding of what's presented in this book and choose between the options for himself.

ADITYA YADAV

Preface

Even though I have known multiple languages since my college days I used them individually on separate projects. 2002 was the first time I used a mix of languages on a single solution this was in Corba, soon after that project I was working with SOA (Service Oriented Architecture) and we used multiple languages. .Net was designed to be language agnostic and always supported multiple languages. And more than anyone would expect developers and architects came with their own biases towards languages. In the last 2 years the JVM has also seen multiple languages being compiled to bytecode and being run on it. We have seen Ruby On Rails being prevalently used. .Net released the Dynamic Language Runtime and we now have a multitude of dynamic languages on it. .Net 4 came with a new first class language called F#. In all it has been a great journey.

During this journey I had a great amount of difficulty in explaining to others why we should go with some language for a particular solution. There were two problems I faced, I wasn't able to articulate well enough to convince them in favor of one language, and the second problem was how much ever I tried they would never agree to adopt a new language because of the learning curve and the effort they would have to put in. I was fired from a few consulting engagements being told that "Polyglots were not needed but rather they needed someone who had focus on one language" something I hear everyday from people who resist change. But the bottomline is that PolyGlots outperform the so called focused language developers in almost everyway.

It is only now I have collected my notes from the last couple of years though in no particular order. I hope readers will find them useful in articulating their arguments for/against different languages and being able to compare different languages and choose the best one(s) for the solution. The problem of converting people into Polyglots still remains. And I would very diplomatically keep my mouth shut on that aspect. 99% of the workforce cannot and will never be Polyglots and there is no use trying to convince them. It is best to present a case before them and hope that reasoning prevails.

ADITYA YADAV

Acknowledgements

Writing this book has been an exciting journey that brought several incredible people together to support me. I would like to thank the knowledgeable reviewers for some of the best feedback during the writing of this book.

I took a sabbatical from work to embark on this journey which has been very fulfilling in many ways. I would like to thank my father Jai Raj Yadav who financially supported me through the sabbatical and with all the resources, travel, household, loan payments and other expenses. Leaving me free to concentrate on nothing but writing the book. I would like to thank my wife Renu for her undivided support during these 4 months. We had a baby boy in Feb 2010 and it has been hard on Renu to leave me alone for long hours undisturbed. She always remembered to serve tea to me every 2 hours all throughout this time, with a smile, I hope I have lived upto her expectations. My 3 year old daughter The Alisha Monster attacks the computer every now and then asking me to show her Disney movies but somehow she has abstained so far. I would like to thank my brother and sister in law Amit and Kalpana, and my mother R.D. Yadav for their faith in me.

I would like to thank the editors who painstakingly proofread the book and the publishers who were all the way through this journey. It is with their help we could together convert a raw idea into a production quality book.

About this book

You may be wondering if there is the need for another book on Programming Languages. I have been programming for the last 15-20 odd years and have used multiple programming languages. This book outlines the concepts and techniques used in implementing programming languages. It doesn't cover X, Y or Z programming language per se. But rather covers the design elements of programming languages in general and sometimes we refer to a particular programming language with examples to explain the concept.

This book is a collection of about 75 chapters which are 1-3 page notes. There is no source code in the book. This book is intended for a technical audience. Though managers and leaders can also read this book to understand the choices their technical folks are making on projects.

Author Online

The resources for this book and the author can be reached at http://adityayadav.com. You can download the last minute changes and errata for the book at the above website. The above website will be accessible as long as the book is in print. Please try the individual language community forums if you have questions specific to a particular language. If the question still remains unanswered please send it to the author through the author's website. The author will answer the questions and also post them on the website for everyone to see. Though this is not a commitment on the part of the author as his contributions to the forum(s) and email responses remain voluntary (and unpaid).

The author has been the CTO of one of the top 25 startups in India dealing with global scale real-time multimedia P2P products. He is also a technology and technology strategy consultant to fortune companies; he provides leadership coaching and architects world class engineering organizations for his clients. He can be reached even outside the context of this book through the author's website.

Imperative Programming Languages

Imperative programming languages are the oldest form of programming languages in the evolution of languages. They started off as assembly and C which were procedural in nature and then moved onto modular and then object oriented programming languages like C++, C#, Java, Ruby etc. These languages are typically those in which a developer specifies how to achieve the result in a step by step fashion. They are lower in evolution. The next step is declarative programming languages where the goals are specified.

Imperative programming languages are identifiable by the set of instructions or commands that ask the computer to perform some action. They have evolved in the level of abstraction over the machine instruction set. They have moved from low level programming of assembly language instructions to compilers which provide higher level API's, libraries and constructs.

Nearly all hardware is designed to execute machine code which is imperative in nature. 1950's saw the development of Algol followed by Cobol, Fortran, Pascal, Basic etc. By default all instructions are executed in a step by step manner, and order of execution is important, unless branching or conditional statements are used. These kind of languages are very difficult to parallelize and execute concurrently. As there is no mechanism by which a compiler or an external tool can take one of these imperative programs and by virtue of some logic transparently convert it into a parallel executing program. Hence we can say that these programming languages cannot be implicitly parallelized. It is the responsibility of the programmer to control the execution of the program and to parallelize it.

Such programs normally don't effectively utilize the current state of multi-core/processor capabilities. Almost 90% of the business systems are made using such languages. The current evolution in microprocessor clock speeds has stagnated. The only way computers will evolve is by adding more and more computing cores/processors to a motherboard/computer.

As a business there is an inherent need for moving onto the next generation of programming languages which are functional, concurrent or declarative in nature. Runtimes like .Net version 4 and JDK 7 have evolved to a state where they are quite effective in utilizing and performing on multiple processors. Tools like databases have also evolved to the stage where they can utilize multiple core computing power. The challenge is for the business to understand which systems and solutions are good to be developed with the basic capabilities of Imperative Languages or if they need the features of more evolved languages. Businesses also will face a lot of issues in finding the right skills to develop newer systems. It is known that professional developers hone only those skills that are in demand. And there is expected to be a lag between the demand for such skills and the supply to catchup.

Functional Programming Languages

Pure functional programming languages are declarative programming languages where the goals to be achieved are declared and not necessarily the step by step procedure to achieve them. Unlike declarative programming languages which specify how to achieve the goals. Some of the earliest languages in this category have been Prolog where the facts were specified and the goal was arrived at by analyzing the facts. Functional programming languages are based on the mathematical concept of a function, avoiding state and mutable data. The difference between the functions used in imperative languages and those in functional languages is that the former can have side effects while the latter usually don't, by which we mean that a function f(x) will have the same output irrespective of the state of the program. This avoids complexities in analyzing the program behavior and allows for easy parallelization as parallel streams work on immutable data and have no side effects and hence don't affect each other and are truly parallelly executable.

Some of the prominent functional programming languages are F#, OCaml, Erlang, Haskell etc. While an imperative language is based on Turing Completeness a functional language is based on Lambda Calculus where a function is denoted by the greek letter Lambda followed by the one character argument name followed by a dot and then the body of the function. E.g. λx.y

All functions with multiple arguments are curryied to arrive at a chain of single argument functions. In the later topics you will see how this is done. This is the most important part of implementation of functional languages. Like Imperative languages functional languages are also translated into an intermediate form. This intermediate form is the lambda calculus notation. Which is then translated into machine code or interpreted.

Concurrent Programming Languages

If you want to create a parallel program in an imperative language then you have to worry about race conditions, locks, semaphores, mutex's, monitors, deadlocks, livelocks etc. A concurrent programming language is one that allows you to create parallel executing programs without worrying about the above, typically all pure functional programming languages without side effects would enable easy concurrent programming. This means functional programming languages are based on functions which work with immutable data and don't modify the input data in any scenario but rather produce new data to be used by the next step of the process; hence these languages are not prone to problems like race conditions, deadlocks, live locks etc.

Many attempts have been made to do concurrent programming using imperative languages by utilizing immutable data structures and deliberately creating functions/subroutines that don't have any side effects, i.e. are not dependant on the state of the program and don't change the state of the program other than producing output based on the input provided to them. While such attempts have succeeded reasonably well, they have done so primarily due to the discipline and expertise of the programmers. The base language or the compiler tools don't provide any features to check a function for side effects in an imperative language or can assist in anyway and it will become increasingly hard to find bugs and analyze these programs. Though Java provides a java.util.concurrent package to aide concurrent programming but I would simply mashup an imperative language along with a concurrent language and use both of them together to make my solution.

It is best to choose a concurrent programming language when the solution demands high amounts or parallelizability and concurrency. The most recent of concurrent programming languages is by Google called Go. The most powerful and perhaps one of the oldest is Erlang which has the best concurrency implementation amongst all known languages, and was originally used in RealTime Telecom applications, internet routers etc.

Domain Specific Languages

A domain specific language is dedicated and usually limited to one problem domain. They may or may not be turing complete, usually not. The best known example of a DSL is SQL which is a language used to work with databases. Just like we embed SQL statements in our programs (most of the times we don't and use an ORM or another abstraction but they in turn will use SQL internally) DSL's generically are also embedded in a program, usually to provide with end user configurability or extensions.

For example a business analyst might utilize the DSL in an insurance product to configure underwriting rules, extend the list of master lookup values or configure notification templates.

Creating a DSL can be a sub-project in itself but is worthwhile as it allows for very powerful system extensions. Very useful for products which need to cater to a wide audience whose needs or patterns of use cannot be anticipated in advance or completely.

Modular & Object Based & Object Oriented Languages

If you see how Basic evolved, it started off as a language with line numbers as Gw-Basic, then came Visual Basic which had the concept of forms and modules which allowed code to be grouped and reused. Then came VB 6 which allowed the use of objects and hence was object based, it encapsulated data and operations inside objects but didn't support inheritance and hence was not truly object oriented. Then came VB.Net 1.1 which was truly object oriented.

Dynamic Programming Languages

.Net 4 has a Dynamic Language Runtime which allows dynamic languages to run on extended CLR. Java 7 is also scheduled to support Dynamic Languages in the runtime. Are dynamic languages anything more than just Dynamically Typed Languages? Yes. Dynamic languages in computer science denote those languages which support most features at runtime which other languages support at compile time, hence making them dynamic. They allow for extending the language by modifying the type system, injecting code, extending objects in ways which usually classes normally are. And the answer to the question is that dynamic languages are usually dynamically typed but not necessarily. Some dynamic languages are Ruby, Python, Groovy etc.

The Microsoft dynamic language runtime is to dynamic languages what CLR was to static languages earlier. It is a common type system and the base framework upon which dynamic languages can be implemented over the CLR, and can interact with statically typed languages and vice versa. This includes dynamic code generation, dynamic method dispatch and the dynamic type system. JDK also supports a similar set of features, invokedynamic, method handles and interface injection. Until JDK 7 comes out running dynamic languages on the JRE would be like fitting square pegs in round holes (i.e. implementing dynamic features over bytecode designed specifically for static languages using workarounds). Post JDK 7 dynamic languages would be first class citizens of the Java world.

Dynamic languages are associated with productivity boosts. Example ruby is supposed to be very easy to develop applications using. Combined with RAD frameworks like Rails allows developers to deliver applications 4-5x times faster to market. While dynamic languages typically lack type safety and all the compiler checks that come along with it. Most of the world has shifted to Agile software development one practice of which is Test Driven Development which involves Unit test code for the functionality developed. TDD coupled with Continous Integration, Automated Builds and Functional Testing allow a thoroughly tested system. This is the argument among dynamic language critics against static language benefits being lost when utilizing dynamic languages.

Multi-Paradigm Programming Languages

There are multiple paradigms a language can address, some of them are imperative, constraint, data flow, object oriented, functional, prototype-based etc.

	C#	Java	Ruby	F#	Python	PHP	C++
Functional	Yes		Yes	Yes	Yes	Yes	
OO	Yes	Yes	Yes	Yes	Yes	Yes	Yes
Imperative	Yes	Yes	Yes	Yes	Yes	Yes	Yes
Generic (Template)	Yes	Yes					Yes
Reflective	Yes	Yes					

What is important to note here that our decision of choosing a primary choice of multi paradigm programming language can be influenced by existing assets to a large extent but leaving that aside C# seems to be the broadest paradigm language. We haven't covered other paradigms but just the top 5 ones.

One of the conclusion from the above table is that language mashups are a necessity. 'Yes' for a language might not necessarily mean that it's a first class concept in that language e.g. functional programming in C#, Ruby, Python are way error prone than in a pure functional language. Likewise imperative programming in F# doesn't gel well with its constructs.

Turing Complete

A programming language is said to be turing complete when its sets of instructions can calculate the result of any function. It has been proven that the only essential condition's to be turing complete is to have conditional branching and being able to manipulate memory.

Turing machines are theoretical machines with infinite amount of RAM and two machines are turing equivalent when they can simulate each other. Most programming languages are Turing Complete. Representations like JSON and XML are not turing complete because they cannot carry instructions and are just a way for representing data.

Turing completeness is a specification of capability rather than a specification of how to achieve that capability. Turing complete languages are said to achieve the results but not how much effort it will require to achieve that result or how much time or memory.

Type System

The Type system of a programming language specifies how first class entities of the language interact with each other and how they can be operated upon and how not. Type checking can be performed at the time of compilation by the compiler in which case it is a static type system or at runtime in which case it is a dynamically typed system. The most common untyped language is assembly language which allows any operation to be performed on any value.

Statically typed languages can be type inferred or manifestly typed. In languages like C# it's a mix of both. In manifestly typed languages every declaration or use needs the type to be indicated. While in cases like lambda expressions in C# the type can be declared or it can be inferred based on usage and context. If it cannot be inferred the compiler throws an exception.

Languages like Ruby allow one variable to refer to data of any type which can be changed at anytime and type checking is performed at runtime. Which leads to the problem of debugging and analyzing type errors in the program.

Weak typing means one type can be used as another in some cases by the use of implicit casts. Strong typed systems prevent any use of a type in a way not consistent with that type. These languages are considered type safe.

	Strongly Typed	Weakly typed
Static Typed	Java	C
Dynamic Typed	Python	PHP

Dynamically Typed Languages

Dynamically typed languages skip type checking at compile time, and perform rather limited type checks even at runtime. They just make sure that the operation is valid. This is usually accompanied by type inference and auto casting from various types into other types. Scala for example is a statically typed language even though it allows you to skip the type declaration. But underneath everything has a static type at compile time. Lisp, perl, python, smalltalk are examples of dynamically typed languages.

Duck Typing

Duck Typing is a style of dynamic typing in which an objects methods and properties define if an operation is valid or not rather than basing the decision on the type of the object. For example in a statically typed language we can have a car object with property engine size and tank size. And another method which prints the engine size and tank size specifies its input parameter as of type 'car'. In a duck typing system there could be any object(s) e.g. Truck and Car which don't have a common super class but have properties defined for engine size and tank size. The method which prints them will specify its input parameter as that of any type as long as it has the tank and engine size properties.

C#, Java as of now have the concept of interfaces which specify the methods supported by the object and many unrelated classes could implement the interface. Operations on these objects can specify the interface as the type for its input parameter. Which in a way brings duck typing to the statically typed world of languages.

The use of 'dynamic' keyword allows for true duck typing in C#, support for Java is due in JDK 7. Critics of duck typing argue that it requires a developer to have broader knowledge of objects and their methods in the system, besides their regular arguments against dynamic programming languages in general. The proponents counter argue that developers should have a global view of the system to be able to develop and maintain it, and to optimize the design and refactor it anyway.

Type Inference

Type inference is another term for implicit typing. This is when you don't explicitly declare the type for a value/object. The compiler can infer the type at compile time from the usage context of that object, if the compiler cannot deduce its type it might throw an error. This eases the programmers job. In cases the compiler cannot deduce the type it will ask the programmer to explicity annotate the object with a type for disambiguation between the one or more types it thinks it could be of.

Hindley-Milner type inference algorithm is the defacto standard algorithm for type inferencing. Which is a rather simple algorithm using which you generate some equations and solve them by unification and substitution to arrive at the most general type for the object.

Type Erasure

Type erasure is one way for language developers to implement generics. Generics in .Net are a part of the runtime which means the executable .Net Assembly supports generics. Java also supports generics but the way it implements them is different, i.e. through type erasure. Which means the java compiler takes a java program which uses generics and transforms it in a way such that it erases all the generics information by replacing them with appropriate casts. The Java runtime and the bytecode hence doesn't see any generics information.

For example the following Java snippet supports generics…

```
List<String> myStrings = new ArrayList<String>();
myStrings.add("One");
myStrings.add("Two");

for (String number : myStrings) System.out.println(number);
```

It gets transformed to the following by the Java compiler…

```
List myStrings = new ArrayList();
myStrings.add((String) "One");
myStrings.add((String) "Two");
for (object number : myStrings) System.out.println((String) number);
```

The java compiler has removed all generics information from the program and placed casts at all the places. The java bytecode has no generics information and inherently doesn't support generics.

Reifiable types are type's whos type information is fully available at runtime. C# uses reification to implement generics such that generics are a first class feature of the language.

Interpreted Languages

The earliest languages were based on an executable program aka interpreter which used to read through the user program kept in a text file one line at a time and execute it. Every possible executable statement had an analogous routine in the interpreter to execute it. If there was a loop every statement in the loop was parsed, an execution graph created and executed which was very tedious. Needless to say such interpreted languages were very slow but they provided a very important developer productivity enhancement by which they allowed in place changes to the user program while debugging and could continue the execution. The developer could even drag the execution pointer to an arbitrary statement and continue execution from there. Every OS the language ran on needed a native interpreter program for that OS to read and execute the user program.

Today most interpreters are in the form of virtual machines which run bytecode which is an intermediate representation of the user program for an abstract machine. The interpreters now don't execute line by line but rather one bytecode instruction at a time. This made it possible for the program syntax to be small and the power of the language was delivered by addon libraries which come along with the interpreter. Such libraries are almost always in the user program language with perhaps some native calls interspersed for native platform capabilities.

Todays interpreters claim near native performance by virtue of pre-compiling the intermediate bytecode into native machine code fragments just in time before execution. This is done by analyzing branch and loop bytecode instructions and compiling code that is expected to be executed just in time. This came along with hardware implementations at the processor level which prefetch program instructions based on anticipated execution paths. About the claim of near native performance, we would say that's not necessarily true.

Interpreted languages like Ruby are preferred by developers because the total time to interpret a ruby program while debugging is lesser than the total time required to compile, build and run and debug a program perhaps in C# delivering enormous improvements in developer productivity. But in most companies it really doesn't matter because some other activity takes an enormous amount of time e.g. working on a remote machine which takes 3-4 minutes to respond, or checking out team source code from the remote VCS which takes 20-30 minutes for a clean checkout.

Compiled Languages

A compiled language e.g. C++ needs a compiler to convert it into a native executable program for a specific operating system. If you see a language like C++ on linux the compiler can generate native programs for multiple hardware configurations. This was achieved by using multiple compiler backends for each target platform. The compiler frontend would parse, analyse and optimize the C++ program while the backend would just be used to emit native executables for a particular hardware configuration. The act of developing a C++ program e.g. on an Intel machine and then generating the executable for e.g. ARM processor was termed cross compilation.

The complete linux operating system was written in a mixture of C and C++ and hence the entire Linux OS source code could be cross compiled for a new hardware, which since it was newly designed didn't have any tooling for it, just by creating a custom C++ compiler backend for that hardware for its instruction set.

If we sit back and think about it one could argue that while we conveniently state that the C++ program is compiled into native machine code, it is actually being interpreted by the processor. We could say that but the generally accepted term is if the hardware is directly executing it, it is considered natively compiled.

There was an interesting development in the world of Pascal about a decade back where in the Pascal compiler could either generate completely native code or it could generate a small native skeleton with a p-language interpreter and the original program could be converted into p-code and put into the native application skeleton. At run time the native skeleton would bootstrap and the p-code interpreter would load the original program in p-code form and execute it.

In java the interpreter is separate from the end user java program, while in .Net the bootstrap hooks the .Net runtime in which then continues the execution of the .Net assembly.

Virtual Machines

Virtual Machines are typically of two types System Virtual Machines and Process Virtual Machines. System Virtual Machines are like VMWare, Xen and VirtualBox they simulate an entire machine while a Process Virtual Machine is meant to run one program in one process. The latter are the kind of virtual machines that execute programming languages. Typically a program is limited to the environment that the virtual machine provides but in the case of Java & .NET virtual machines there are native API's JNI and P/Invoke respectively that allow the program to access the environment outside the Process Virtual Machine on the physical operating system and hardware. System Virtual Machines are used to virtualize enterprise infrastructure and they work together along with virtualized storage and virtualized networking.

Process Virtual Machines are used to distribute and run programs in an architecture neutral format. This means that the program is converted into a virtual instruction set which the virtual machine executes. VM's come with an elaborate toolset which allow such architecture independent programs to be compiled to the native platform. Typically the VM will come with a tool to compile the program into a virtual executable format. The virtual machine then runs the program by interpreting the architecture independent executable format.

There are two prevalent designs of Virtual Machines, ones based on stack architecture and ones based on register architecture. To execute an instruction requires three steps fetching the instruction from memory, fetching the operands and executing the instruction. A typical stack based implementation would load operand(s) onto the stack, pop the operands and perform the instruction and store the result back on the stack, in a typical task. While a register implementation would execute a simple task in one go as 'IADD r,a,b'. It is known that a virtual register based VM performs lesser dispatches than a stack based one. The actual dispatch is performed in a large switch case statement, with one case for each operand. The alternative to switch case implementation is a 'threaded dispatch'.

The other operation is fetching operands. In a stack based machine the operands are located relative to the stack pointer, which in a register based machine are located absolutely in memory. An average register instruction is longer than the stack one. And small code and less number of memory fetches are the reasons stack based machines are developed. Also pretty much every physical machine has a stack but its registers differ a lot. Hence a stack based implementation makes a lot of sense in terms of being able to abstract physical machines.

While a virtual machine interprets the architecture independent program bytecode/executable and hence is inherently slower than native programs. Improvements in Just in Time Compilation techniques have bridged the gap largely.

Two of the most famous Virtual Machines are the JVM (Java Virtual Machine) and the .NET CLR (Common Language Runtime). Both are based on the Stack architecture. The Java Compiler compiles the Java program to an intermediate format called Java ByteCode. Originally JVM was meant for only the Java language, many languages like Scala, Groovy, JavaScript, Python can now be compiled into Java ByteCode. While the CLR was meant to be a language neutral architecture from the beginning. The JVM is inherently statically typed which means it was meant for statically typed languages. Dynamic language support is forecasted to be available in JDK 7.

.NET programs get compiled into IL (Intermediate Language) which along with Metadata make assemblies. Just In Time compilation converts the IL into native executable code which is then executed. There is no interpretation; hence .Net programs are generally faster than Java programs. .Net CLR is designed as a host to many languages e.g. C#, J#, C++/CLI, VB.Net and now is also capable of running Dynamic Languages with the Dynamic Language Runtime.

Other things that come along with a virtual machine are memory management, security, and platform independence. In some cases the VM can JIT compile a program more optimally according to the exact hardware than native programs compiled for a specific hardware family.

Inheritance

Single inheritance is a mechanism in which one class can inherit from only one another class. In multiple inheritance one class can inherit from multiple other classes. The latter leads to a couple of problems (1) how are the constructors chained and in which order so as to create a consistent subclass object? (2) what methods are inherited from which super classes? Inheritance allows you to write code for a generic case and another developer to write code for more specialized cases such that both pieces of code continue to function unbroken. The derived type acts just like its parent except for specializations it brings in along with any extensions it adds. Normally there is no way to remove a feature unless you override the feature with a blank implementation. Single inheritance forms a inheritance tree while multiple inheritance forms a directed acylic inheritance graph.

Inheritance increases software reuse and quality. Deep hierarchies can complicate development though, which works easier in case of single inheritance which itself could get complicated but multiple inheritance hierarchies can get incomprehensible and unmanageable. That what is not understood is not used leading to patchwork of inconsistent code. Deep hierarchies have a slight performance impact due to dynamic binding not noticeable mostly but nevertheless. Inheritance enables the "Open for extension closed for modification" software development principle.

A couple of strategies were used to solve these problems. One way is to specify which parent class the feature should come from e.g. in C++ you can specify feature by feature the parent class of the feature. E.g. Ocaml automatically takes the feature from the last class mentioned in the list of parent classes which have the feature. In case you want to use a feature from another parent class you would have to qualify the method call with the name of the parent class.

Such languages leave the management of inheritance hierarchy on the developer. Later languages like C# and Java evolved using a simpler mechanism which guaranteed consistency and zero ambiguities at the compile time. They used interfaces which are skeletons with method signatures. The subclass can inherit from one class and one class only but implement multiple interfaces. The developer has to put in the implementations of the methods in the interface definitions by hand. The constructor of the superclass can be called using the super keyword or a qualifier. And similarly the super class methods can also be referenced in the subclass using the keyword or a qualifier. This leaves no ambiguity at the compile time and this bypasses complicated mechanisms in earlier languages.

An alternative to inheritance is object composition, in which we create a new class with multiple objects referred of the classes we need. The new class then proxies methods to use these objects and orchestrates them to achieve the desired result.

Syntactic Sugar

Syntactic sugar is something which is not a part of the language kernel. It is merely something that exists as an easy way of representing or doing something. There are multiple views on it Ruby on one hand tries to stay clear of syntactic sugar while .Net has them in abundance. Some techies think that it increases the learning curve and makes understanding the code difficult.

One such example is properties in .Net. If you see Getters and Setters that you would have written for them earlier you would have written something like

```
public string _Name;
public string Name {
        get {
                return _Name;
        }
        set {
                _Name = value;
        }
}
```

In later versions of .Net we could do the same with just

```
public string Name {get; set;}
```

Other examples are Lambda Expressions, Implicitly Typed Locals, Anonymous Types, Object/Collection Initializers, Partial Classes etc.

Partial Classes

Partial Classes are a mechanism whereby an actual class is split into multiple files. The compiler actually does a precompilation phase where it assembles the class from multiple files before compiling it. This is a syntactic sugar and in many ways is very useful for separation of concerns, allowing multiple developers to work on different parts of the code.

.Net compiler supports Partial Classes. You can see in the Solution Explorer that there are files like Form1.cs and Form1.Designer.cs when you are designing forms. The designer generates code into the Form1.Designer.cs file while you are meant to only put code in Form1.cs file. Java doesn't have any feature like this and Form designers in Java/Swing etc. usually fallback to keeping a generated file which contains the form metadata and the actual .java files has both generated sections and developer code.

Partial Methods

Partial methods are a feature of C# language version 3 and go hand in hand with Partial Classes which came in C# version 2 (VB.Net implied) Partial methods can exist only inside partial classes but unlike partial classes they don't split one method into two parts but rather they allow for absence of implementation of a method. A partial method cannot return anything, has a void return type and cannot have out parameters. They cannot be called from outside the class and have no access specifiers. They allow end user extensions to a class by providing implementations for the partial method. If the implementation is not provided the compiler will show no trace of the partial method or any calls to it as if it never existed.

Example

```
partial class DemoClass {
        private int i;
        public DemoClass(int i){
                this.i = i;
// this statement will vanish from IL if impl. doesn't exist @ compilation
                LogTheValue(i);
        }
        partial void LogTheValue(int i);
}

partial class DemoClass {
        partial void LogTheValue(int i){
                Console.WriteLine("Value of i="+i.ToString());
        }
}
```

Now try to visualize its importance in this way. The first partial class is autogenerated by some code generation tool and it makes a call to a partial method LogTheValue(i) which is not implemented in the generated code. Lets say the code generator is an off the shelf tool provided by a vendor.

As a developer you cannot touch the generated code because your changes will get overwritten the next time the code is regenerated. What you can do is to implement the partial method in the other partial class which is used for developer code. If you don't implement the partial method the compiler will remove the partial method and all calls to it from the generated IL and it will not be a part of the executable as if it never existed.

Lambda Expressions

A lambda expression is an anonymous function that can contain expressions and statements. C# supports lambda expressions where the lambda operator has the input parameters if any to its left and the expression or the statement to its right.

```
delegate int mydelegate(int x, int y);
delegate void myconsolelogger(string someText);
void MyMethod()
{
    mydelegate sumOfSquares = (int x,int y) => x*x+y*y;
    int result = sumOfSquares(2,3)); //result = 13
    myconsolelogger myConsoleLogger = (string x) =>{ string toPrint = "Log:"+x; Console.WriteLine(toPrint);
};
    myConsoleLogger("Program completed");
}
```

Closures

In programming languages a closure is said to occur when a function references variables of an outer scope. The variables are used by the function for the term of its life. In Java we can see this happen with anonymous classes bound to variables from an outer higher scope.

// as long as MyListener lives it will be able to use the name and length variables.

```
public void mymethod(final String name){
        final int length = name.length();
        lib.setListener(new MyListener(){
                public void printEverything(){
                        System.out.println("Name: "+name+"is of length:"+length);
                }
        });
        ...
        lib.printEverything();// calls the MyListener and prints everything
}
```

Closures defer execution. They are best used to implement control structures in the language. For example an if-then statement shown below

```
if (x>5){
        print("x is greater than 5");
}else {
        print("x is less than or equal to 5");
}
```

Can be implemented using 3 closures.

```
{ return x>5}, { print("x is greater than 5");}, { print("x is less than or equal to 5");}
```

which are bound to the variable x from the outer scope. The first closure evaluating the condition and the other two executing its branches.

Higher Order Functions

Higher order functions are functions that can take other functions as input or return functions as output. **First class** functions are functions that can appear anywhere in a program as a first class element of that program and hence forth it is also a higher order function as it can also appear as an input into a function or as the output of a function.

Typically First Class functions are implemented as a function type which is at par with other types like Float and Int.

Currying

Currying is a simplification mechanism which can be used only in the presence of higher order functions. When a function has 'n' arguments. It processes the first argument and returns a function which processes the next argument which returns a function which processes the next argument and so on. Converting an 'n' dimensional function in to a chain of 'n' single dimension functions.

Example $F(x,y)= x^2 + y^3$

For $F(5,6) = G(6)$ where $G(y) = y^3+25$

This results in simplified evaluations.

Also in the case of example $F(x,y) = y * x$++

We have $F(2,3)= G(3)$ where $G(y) = \{ x=2+1; return\ 2*y \}$

Now if we see how this simplifies expression evaluation which uses side effects like x++.

Uncurrying is the transformation of a chain of curried functions taking one argument at a time into one single function which does the same thing and returns the same result but takes all the arguments in one go.

Partial Application

Partial application is when you supply lesser than required arguments to the function. The function then partially applies the arguments it has received and returns a function that accepts the rest of the arguments which were not supplied.

For e.g $F(a,b,c,d) = a^2 + b^3 + c^4 + d^5$

$F(2,3,,)$ gives $G(c,d)$ where $G(c,d) = 4+9+c^4 + d^5$

The order of parameters matters and the omitted parameters generally come later.

Function Composition

Function composition is the act of chaining one or more functions so that the results of one function are input to the next function. This is usually implemented by some sort of a pipe operator. The basic idea is to create new and powerful functions based on other functions.

This is analogous to the idea of object oriented inheritance.

e.g.

```
let getFolderSize =
   filesUnderFolder
   >> Seq.map fileInfo
   >> Seq.map fileSize
   >> Seq.fold (+) 0L
   >> bytesToMB
let photosInMB_funccomp = getFolderSize @"C:\Users\aditya\Documents\"
```

Memoization

Memoization is a specific term for functions on lines of caching in applications. To implement memoization we implement caching in a function such that the function remembers which inputs result in which outputs so that it returns the output from the cache rather than performing the calculation each time. It is a given that memoization is useful only when a couple of conditions hold true.

1) Memoization takes dramatically lesser time than performing the calculation.

2) The calculation in the function is not affected by any state of the program and only depends on the inputs and produces the same output irrespective of the state of the program, i.e. no side effects.

3) Cache can grow out of control and there is a simple mechanism to manage the cache.

4) The Cache should ideally be distributed between machines running the function

5) An algorithm can be used to maximize cache hits with minimum cache size

Language Workbenches

Language workbenches are tools/IDE's that help you extend a language by creating DSL's. Which are broadly categorized into two types; external DSL's are usually made in another language and generate code for a different target language while internal DSLs share the same language as the target language and are more tightly integrated with the target.

Two most common language workbenches at the time of this writing are from Intentional Softwares and JetBrains. While DSLs is nothing unusual for developers. The language workbenches are targeted also at the business domain experts who can express concepts, rules and constraints using the Workbench (which together will be called their business domain language) which can then be 'projected' into code, screens or sql etc.

Generics

While C# and .Net in general has specific instructions in the compiled code to represent Generic type information. The Java bytecode has no trace of generic type information as it implements generics through a compiler trick called type erasure.

This basically means that you cannot overload Java methods with generic types e.g.

In java you cannot have both

public void doSomething(List<String> myList){}

public void doSomething(List<Integer> myList){}

while you can have both these methods in .Net as the it considers both to be different while Java will translate both to

public void doSomething(List myList){}

public void doSomething(List myList){}

Using type erasure i.e. using casts everywhere 'myList' is accessed in the function, and the Java compiler will throw an exception in the above scenario.

Polymorphic Types

In Java and C# all types inherit from the root class Object and hence if you specify a return type as Object (Polymorphic Return Types) you can return any type. In languages where this is not possible polymorphic types are implemented using a wrapper which is a composite of many types that are relevant in that context. This is also valid for input parameter types.

e.g.

```
class PaymentInformation {
        constant int CreditCardType = 0;
        constant int PayPalType = 1;
        int chosenInformationType;
        PayPalInformation payPalInformation;
        CreditCardInformation creditCardInformation;
}
...
public PaymentInformation GetPaymentInformation(int accountID){
        if (accounted >0){
                return PaymentInformationFactory.GetInstance().getPayMentInformation( accounted);
        }else {
                return null;
        }
}
...
public void MakePayment(PaymentInformation payInfo, int amount){
        IPaymentFactory= PaymentFactory.GetInstance(payInfo.chosenInformationType);
        IPaymentFactory.MakePayment(payInfo, amount);
}
```

A function that can process polymorphic types is also called a **Polymorphic Function**. When heterogeneous types are used uniformly they are termed adhoc type polymorphism. When there is a common root class to all the types e.g. in Java and C# it is called inclusion polymorphism. When the language doesn't have any type information associated with the parameters e.g. in dynamic languages then it is termed as parametric polymorphism.

Co-variance & Contra-variance

A type system is covariant if it orders types from more specific to more generic. E.g. if a function returns a type of class A and it is allowed to return either an instance of class A or any subtype of A e.g. if B extends A then it is co-variant.

A type system is contra-variant if it is the opposite of co-variant and orders types from more generic to more specific. Most languages have features which are covariant or contravariant in specific contexts and it is important to understand which way in which context.

In C# and Java arrays are covariant

String[] a = new String[]{"name"};

e.g. object[] b = a;

is valid, but this leads to type unsafety as you can treat a String array as an object array and insert objects of types other than string into it by mistake and have a runtime exception processing the array. Generically speaking in a write environment contravariance is safe while covariance is not.

Delegates in C# are both covariant and contravariant i.e. they can have covariant return types and contravariant argument types. Languages are generally return type covariant.

IEnumerable<T> (T is covariant)

IEnumerator<T> (T is covariant)

IQueryable<T> (T is covariant)

IGrouping<TKey, TElement> (TKey and TElement are covariant)

IComparer<T> (T is contravariant)

IEqualityComparer<T> (T is contravariant)

IComparable<T> (T is contravariant)

Reflection

Reflection is the feature in programming languages that allows the programmer to inspect and manipulate code entities without knowing their identification or formal structure ahead of time. Inspection entails analyzing objects and types to gather structured information about their definition and behavior. Typically this is done with little or no prior knowledge about them, apart from some basic provisions. Manipulation uses the information gained through inspection to invoke code dynamically, create new instances of discovered types, or even restructure types and objects on the fly.

Both Java and C# used to support reflection dynamically. You had to specify the class name for example as a string and you could get its information and you could provide the name of a method as a string and you could get its information and invoke it. This is the classic implementation of reflection in languages.

Dynamic reflection is very refactoring non-friendly, i.e. if you rename the method you will have to manually change the string in the reflecting code, and features like Intellisense don't work with it.

Static reflection on the other hand doesn't use Magic Strings but rather uses Lambda Expressions e.g. e => e.MyProperty

Introspection

Introspection is the capability of a language to determine the type of an object at runtime. Typically in java this is done as

if (myobject instanceof String){...}

in C# this is done using 'is' and 'as' e.g.

if (myobject is String){...}

or

String myObjectAsString = myobject as String;

If (myObjectAsString != null) {...} // its of type String

Ruby has methods 'instance_of' and 'kind_of' methods to determine the type of any object.

Operator Overloading

Critics of the Java language argue that Java doesn't feature operator overloading because it can lead to confusing code, though it is implemented for the String object as an exception as it makes intuitive sense to the developers.

Operator Overloading sometimes referred to as operator ad-hoc polymorphism refers to operators like +, -, *, / having different implementation depending on the type used in the context of the operation. Which means if + is used between integers it will sum the integer, if it used between String's it will concatenate the strings, if it is used between a developer defined custom type it will perform the operation on the two objects as per the '+' operator overloading definition created by the developer.

In C# all unary, binary and relational operators can be overloaded. see example below.

```
public class Point {
...
public static Point operator -(Point p)
{
        Point temp = new Point();
        temp.x = this.x - p.x;
        temp.y = this.y - p.y;
        return temp;
}
...
}
...
Point result = new Point(3,4) - new Point (1,2);
```

Garbage Collection

Most virtual machines provide managed memory features. Which means when a new object is created it is allocated memory from the managed heap and when the object is destroyed the memory is reclaimed. But most VMs go a step further by implementing garbage collection algorithms by which they automatically try to infer which objects are not needed and hence are garbage and can be reclaimed. To do this the VM has to keep track of the use of objects, we can say if there are one or more valid references to an object it is still needed, so VM's have algorithms around counting references, multiple allocation and de-allocation of objects in memory can also fragment the heap and it may also need to be compacted and objects moved around. How do you actually move around objects without halting the program, most VMs create one level of indirection between the reference and the pointer to the object by using an intermediate variable. So basically the object reference points to an internal variable which in turn points to the object. But not everything can be done without impacting the performance of the running application. Even counting references to an object takes a sizeable overhead.

Most garbage collection algorithms divide the heap into generations each of which store objects of the same age of number of GC cycles they have been through. Statistically objects which have longer age tend to stay on longer and objects freshly created tend to get destroyed quickly. A GC cycle will also call the finalizers on objects before garbage collecting them which also causes delays and performance hits. There are broadly two categories of GC algorithms ones that pause the application and perform the GC i.e. stop the world/synchronous and ones that continue to do their work slowly along with the application i.e. concurrent.

Garbage Collection algorithms are compared based on application pause times, performance impact and predictability. .Net 4 has added various events in relation with GC which the application code can hook onto. Both .Net 4 and JDK 7 have improved concurrent GC algorithms that perform well with multi-core systems which otherwise would have degraded the system to 40% throughput using previous algorithms with e.g. 32 processors.

Continuations

When continuations are implemented every function takes another argument which is its continuation. This eliminates extra control flows like try/catch and if-then-else statements and also enables asynchronous programming.

For example a regular function F(x,y)=x+y

When using continuations will be implemented as

F(x,y,continuation) and now this function F will run and calculate a result which is x+y and pass this result to the continuation which can further process the result.

If you have seen Ajax calls every ajax call can use a continuation which can process the result of making the call to the server. This is the most common application of continuations i.e. in asynchronous programming.

Weak References

A weak reference is a reference to an object that doesn't prevent that object to be collected by the garbage collector. A strong reference is the normal reference to an object when it is used as by a variable, as a parameter etc. As long as there is a strong reference to an object it will not be garbage collected by the garbage collector.

Creating excess objects or not dereferencing objects after they are not needed can lead to memory leaks. Memory leaks can also occur when a group of otherwise unreachable objects have references to each other.

A soft reference is usually used to implement a cache in which when memory starts getting full objects are automatically removed. While soft referenced objects get collected only if there is an impending need due to low memory. Weak referenced objects are garbage collected when all other strong references to it cease to exit. This is useful when an object/resource is distributed by a module which is expected to be returned after its use is finished. When the resource is not explicitly returned but its use has ceased and hence all references to it have been removed it can be finalized and garbage collected and accounted for by the module.

C# and Java both support weak references while Java also supports soft and phantom references. All of weak, soft and phantom references are collectively sometimes referred to as weak references which could be confusing.

Platform Independence

A platform independent software is one which doesn't depend on native features of any platform. While 'cross platform' software are those which use native features of different platforms but do it in such a way that it abstracts away the platform dependencies and makes the features available in a way that programmers don't need to think about specific platform features but rather work with an abstracted API. When the software runs on platform 'a' it binds to its native features and when on 'b' it binds to b's native features without requiring any changes to the program.

Let's take the example of Java its runtime takes care of running java programs on Linux and Windows. But the java program developer doesn't need to know about the underlying OS he programs in java using an abstracted windowing library e.g. Swing and the runtime will hook onto the native OS to execute the windowing features.

Platform independent toolkits, frameworks and languages typically provide a common minimum subset of all the platforms. While cross platform tools, frameworks can support the full native features of all platforms but with perhaps using multiple code bases or some part of the developers codebase specific to a platform and conditionally compiled to create a build targeted specifically for that platform, while the rest of the codebase is platform agnostic and uses fallbacks for features not supported by the underlying platform.

Arbitrary Precision Arithmetic

Arbitrary precision arithmetic means being able to perform mathematical operations to an infinite number of decimal places, as many as required by the calculations; limited only by the memory in the system.

Just about a decade ago there was a special ALU chip on the motherboard of computers which specialized in mathematical operations. Today it is done by the cpu core itself. But the way it works has not changed much. Every number is stored in the registers and the instruction then operates on the registers and stores the results in another register or memory location. The size of integers and floating point numbers on the hardware are limited by the register size. This is termed as fixed precision arithmetic.

There are some machines which support arbitrary precision arithmetic's at the hardware level, but generally it is implemented in software and hence is considerably slow. Both Java and .Net support arbitrary precision arithmetic. In most cases where this is needed speed is not a limiting factor but rather it is important that the result be accurate to the required decimal places.

Languages that support hardware abstraction also implement a modified version of arbitrary precision arithmetic. They have fixed precisions that are defined for an abstract machine. If the precision is supported by the hardware it gets executed natively on the hardware or else it is simulated in software. This allows for hardware agnostic implementation of languages in Java and C# unlike languages like C++.

Meta Programming

Meta programming is the mechanism of writing programs to write end user programs. It's also called as code-generation. The simplest use case for which is when the program contains a lot of boiler plate code, then it can be meta programmed. Attempts to generate business logic with meta programming have failed till now and this should be avoided.

Typically developers create the first few pieces of similar code manually and then create a meta program template for it which is then used to generate the rest of the code similar to the one created manually.

Meta programming seems to have originated with Lisp. "In Lisp, you don't just write your program down toward the language, you also build the language up toward your program."- Paul Graham

Ruby seems to be the next best widely used alternative to Lisp for meta programming. It allows easy development of DSLs which comes naturally to dynamic languages.

Mixins

Ruby mixins are the best implementation of mixins. Generally languages provide classes and interfaces while ruby provides classes, modules and mixins which are a mix of classes and modules. With a mixin you can extend a module rather than from a class.

Modules can be mixed with a class using the 'extend' or 'include' mechanism. The include method will mix a module's methods at the instance level, meaning that the methods of the module will become instance methods. While extend method will mix a module at the class level and the methods defined in the module will become class level or static methods.

Some languages don't allow multiple inheritance unlike C++ and rather support Classes and Interfaces. Designers of ruby too decided not to support multiple inheritance and created the mixin mechanism for developers to be able to include code from a module into a class statically or at the instance level.

Because of the mixin feature developers can include arbitrary code into an extended class which is very powerful if you are trying to create plugins or extensions to a framework.

Tail Recursion

Tail recursion is a special case of recursion where the last call in the function is recursive. Recursion works by utilizing the stack and it can easily fillup and overflow the stack, in the special case of tail recursion, it can be easily and automatically be converted into an iterative implementation saving the stack space.

For example:

```
int factorial(x){
        if (x==0) {
                return 1;
        } else {
                return x*factorial(x-1);
        }
}
```

Is an example of tail recursion with only the last call being recursive. It can automatically be converted into the following non-stack based iterative implementation as follows.

```
int factorial(x){
        int result = 1;
        for (int i=x; i>=0;x--){
                result = result * x;
        }
        return result;
}
```

Tail recursion saves not only stack space and memory by utilizing iteration along with an accumulator but they also prevent from problems of implementing deep recursive procedures without sufficient memory.

Pattern Matching

Most functional programming languages like ML, Erlang, OCaml, F# have some or the other form of pattern matching. Pattern matching is more than a switch statement in the sense that it can support ranges, all types rather than just primitive types, test for state etc.

```
let rec fib n =
  match n with
  | x when x < 0 -> failwith "value must be greater than or equal to 0"
  | 0 | 1 -> 1
  | x -> fib(n - 2) + fib(n - 1)
```

The above is a very compact representation of a Fibonacci function which uses pattern matching. The above function fails with an exception if the parameter is less than 0. For 0 or 1 it returns 1 and for anything above that it returns the actual value through recursive calls.

F# has an extensible pattern matching syntax called active patterns which allows F# to work smoothly with OO constructs. Which is said to be particularly useful while implementing parsers.

Runtime Evaluation

Most interpreted languages provide some sort of a 'eval' function which takes a text/string of code block and executes it. Runtime evaluation comes very naturally to scripted and interpreted languages.

Compiled languages implement Runtime Evaluation through mechanisms available in the runtime e.g. reflection, bytecode generation/compilation, dynamic program loading. Which in essence are put together to compile a small snippet of the program usually in memory, loaded and executed. Such that the context can be transferred from the parent program to the evaluated snippet and results brought back.

Runtime evaluation is the first step to creating extensible programs without creating a custom DSL and its execution engine.

REPL

REPL = Read-Eval-Print-Loop

A REPL implementation is usually a console program which allows code snippets to be entered and executed. The code snippets usually print something to the console. REPL consoles where available are an incredibly productivity enhancer and an essential part of the developer toolbox.

Typical uses of a REPL console are for debugging code snippets, development of code fragments which otherwise would require the entire build process to do and perhaps a lot of plumbing.

REPL which is almost always available for scripting languages is also available for compiled languages like Java, C# and F#. This brings benefits of interpreted languages to compiled languages amongst other things.

Static and Dynamic Scoping

Every entity in a programming language has a context inside which it is valid e.g. a variable could have function level scope, instance level scope, class level scope or global scope. When definitions of entities overlap across scopes the actual use of the entity requires a resolution of the scope to which it applies and there are rules in the language for it.

Static scoping also called as Lexical scoping is determined at compile time. It has no runtime overhead and the desired outcome can be validated by looking at the program structure. Dynamic scoping on the other hand is determined at the runtime based on the call hierarchy which can only be determined at the runtime. Which could depend on the exact execution path which cannot be determined at compile time and hence at runtime there is an overhead to resolve the value of an identifier.

Prototype Based Language

Prototype based languages don't have the concept of classes and objects they simply have objects which extend code and data from other object templates. Java script is a prototype based language.

JavaScript implements inheritance by allowing you to associate a prototypical object with any constructor function. In javascript you can add/remove properties to objects at runtime which is not possible in class based languages. Which have a separate class definition based on which objects are instantiated. A prototype-based language, such as JavaScript, does not make this distinction: it simply has objects. A prototype-based language has the notion of a prototypical object, an object used as a template from which to get the initial properties for a new object. Any object can specify its own properties, either when you create it or at run time. In addition, any object can be associated as the prototype for another object, allowing the second object to share the first object's properties.

In javascript if you add/remove properties to the prototype object all the objects that are based on it get affected.

Variadic Functions

There are some operations in programs which could use any number of arguments. Functions which accept variable number of arguments are also called as variadic functions. Operations like sum/average of numbers or string concatenation are such examples. Almost all languages like Java, C#, List, Haskell, Php, Perl, Python have implementations of variadic functions.

e.g. Java

```
public void printEverything(String... strings) {
  for (String s : strings)
    System.out.print(s + " ");
}
```
e.g. in C#

```
public void PrintEverything(params String[] strings)
{
   foreach (String s in strings)
      Console.Write(s + " ");
}
```

Checked Exceptions

A checked exception is one that is declared in the method signature and has to be either passed on by the calling method or handled appropriately.

While an unchecked exception need not be declared in the signature or handled by the calling method. In the event it remains unhandled it will stop the program or thread.

Java supports both checked and unchecked exceptions while C# only supports unchecked exceptions. While C# programs don't look cluttered and have simpler method signatures, developers cannot throw custom exceptions. There is no way for one to know what exceptions a method will throw and probably need to be handled unless you have the source code for the method or the original developer has documented it. But then it also leads to a simpler exception handling at the caller end by created a catch all exception which says "Operation Failed: Trying to do 'xyz'"

Before the advent of exceptions as a language feature all error handling was done by method return codes, remember C?

Deterministic Disposal

Typically a lot of code was put in destructors of the class to release resources e.g. in C++ and a manual mechanism was provided to call the destroy method on the object instance. This was pretty deterministic as in you could control when the resources are released. With the advent of languages like Java and C# which had automatic garbage collection you couldn't control when the destructor would be called. This led to the practice of avoiding the use of destructors and releasing resources just after they were used.

Managed resources are disposed off when they are not referenced anymore and they are not usually a problem. Finalizers are used to dispose off unmanaged resources. The Dispose pattern if properly implemented guarantees deterministic disposal of unmanaged resources and if the developer forgets calling it then they will definitely be disposed by the garbage collector.

e.g. of Dispose pattern in C# (paraphrased from MSDN)

```
// Design pattern for a base class.
public class Base: IDisposable
{
  //Implement IDisposable.
  public void Dispose()
  {
   Dispose(true);
    GC.SuppressFinalize(this);
  }

  protected virtual void Dispose(bool disposing)
  {
    if (disposing)
    {
      // Free other state (managed objects).
    }
    // Free your own state (unmanaged objects).
    // Set large fields to null.
  }

  // Use C# destructor syntax for finalization code.
  ~Base()
```

```
  {
    // Simply call Dispose(false).
    Dispose (false);
  }

// Design pattern for a derived class.
public class Derived: Base
{
  protected override void Dispose(bool disposing)
  {
    if (disposing)
    {
      // Release managed resources.
    }
    // Release unmanaged resources.
    // Set large fields to null.
    // Call Dispose on your base class.
    base.Dispose(disposing);
  }
  // The derived class does not have a Finalize method
  // or a Dispose method with parameters because it inherits
  // them from the base class.
}
```

C# provides deterministic disposal while Java does not.

Conditional Compilation

Conditional Compilation was implemented decades back in C/C++ so that a piece of code/snippet could be compiled depending on whether a value was present or not. This allowed developers to implement platform specific code and create builds targeted for one of the many platforms while keeping a single codebase. It allowed the developer to create a debug build with debug statements interspersed within the production code marked by conditional compilation directives.

The way conditional compilation was implemented was using compiler pre-processor directives. The compiler used to analyze and process the pre-processor directives and create a substituted code file which was subsequently compiled.

e.g. to insert debug statements

```
#ifdef DEBUG
printf("x is %d\n", x);
#endif
```

e.g. to compile selectively for 32 or 64 bit platforms

```
#ifdef WIN32
// Win32 code
#else
// Win64 code
#endif
```

IE supported conditional compilation of JScript/JavaScript since the IE4 days. the example below prints if Java Script version is greater than 5 or not.

```
/*@cc_on
  @if (@_jscript_version >= 5)
    document.write("JScript version >= 5");
  @else
    document.write("JScript version < 5");
  @end
```

@*/

PL/SQL also supports conditional compilation. See example below

```
$IF boolean_static_expression $THEN text
  [ $ELSIF boolean_static_expression $THEN text ]
  [ $ELSE text ]
$END
```

Object Pinning

C# provides a keyword 'fixed' which tells the .Net runtime garbage collector to not move the object around in memory which it normally can and does during garbage collection. This is primarily used when the managed code makes a call to a native method which uses a local variable, and hence the local object should not be moved around, even if the garbage collection kicks in, as long the native call is in progress.

Fixing a lot of objects over extended periods of time can cause heap fragmentation. Hence objects should be pinned only when absolutely necessary and for the shortest period of time required. If the native method caches the pointer and then the object is unpinned and consequently moved by the garbage collector the program will crash on the callback from the native method.

e.g. of object pinning in C#

```
Point pt = new Point( 3,4);
fixed ( int* p = &pt.x )
{
    // make the native  call passing 'p'
}// p is unpinned anytime beyond this closing bracket
```

Inner Classes

Inner classes are nested classes inside another class. They allow all the more structuring of code beyond what classes and inheritance mechanisms provide. An inner class is associated with the containing class and cannot exist outside it, and has access to all the members of the containing class.

An anonymous inner class is an inner class without a name usually used to implement callbacks.

```
button.addActionListener(new ActionListener() {
        public void actionPerformed(ActionEvent e) {
                System.out.println("The button was pressed!");
        }
});
```

Some people like to look at inner classes as syntactic sugar.

Enumerations

An enumeration associates names with an underlying type, usually signed and unsigned integer, and has fields. It is different from a struct in the sense that it cannot contain methods or implement interfaces normally.

e.g. a classic enumeration in C# with byte as the underlying type

```
public enum Fruits : byte
{
    Apple,
    Mango,
    Orange,
    Banana
}
```

Bit enumerations are also implemented sometimes when flags are needed.

e.g in C#

```
[Flags]
public enum Fruits
{
    None = 0,
    Apple = 1,
    Mango = 2,
    Orange = 4,
    Banana = 8,
    All = Apple | Mango | Orange | Banana
}
…
Fruits myFruits = Apple | Mango;
```

Explicit Pointer

Most managed languages have implicit pointers e.g. in Java super and this point to the parent or self. Every variable in e.g. Java is a pointer to the object but you cannot create one explicitly, the pointers are implicit as in you can manipulate the objects but not play around with the pointers to the objects which are implicit i.e. no pointer arithmetic.

Explicit pointers are used for dynamic memory allocation probably contigous, explicit memory management and accessing native libraries and features of the platform. Common problems with explicit pointers are

1- Dangling pointers – When the object to which the pointer points has been deallocated, typically happens when multiple pointers point to the object and the object has been deallocated using one pointer.

2- Memory leaks – When objects are lost when pointers get reassigned multiple times to other objects losing references to previous objects which stay on the heap even though they are not referenced anymore.

3- Double deallocation – When the dynamic heap object is deallocated more than once corrupting the heap.

4- Aliasing – When multiple pointers point to the same shared resource, changing the resource using one pointer causes the other program units to be non-locally affected as a side effect.

Virtual Methods

Virtual methods are those methods which can be overridden by the subclass. Typically methods which have a modifier such as 'virtual' can be overridden. Typically while overriding in the subclass a modifier on the method such as 'override' states that the intent is to override the method with the same signature in the parent class. A non-virtual method is invariant. In java every non-static method is virtual unless marked with 'final' in which case it cannot be overridden.

In C# while invoking a virtual method the runtime type of the object determines the method invoked. While in a non-virtual method invocation the compile time type decides which method is invoked.

```
class B
{
   public void MyNonVirtual() { Console.WriteLine("B:MyNonVirtual"); }
   public virtual void MyVirtual() { Console.WriteLine("B:MyVirtual"); }
}
class D: B
{
   new public void MyNonVirtual() { Console.WriteLine("D:MyNonVirtual"); }
   public override void MyVirtual() { Console.WriteLine("D:MyVirtual"); }
}
class LetsFigureThingsOut
{
   static void Main() {
      D d = new D();
      B b = d;
      b.MyNonVirtual();
      d.MyNonVirtual();
      b.MyVirtual();
      d.MyVirtual();
   }
}

prints

B:MyNonVirtual
D:MyNonVirtual
D:MyVirtual
D:MyVirtual
```

When it comes to calling non virtual methods in the above case the compile time type for b is B (base class) while for d is D (derived class) and hence two different methods are called.

In the case of virtual methods the runtime type for b and d is always D (derived class) which is the type of the actual derived class object and hence in both cases the virtual method gets called.

Dynamic Dispatch

Method invocation can happen with early binding or late binding. Based on the runtime type of the object which can always only be known at the runtime the actual decision to call which method (parent class or subclass) method is made. This is done using dynamic dispatch or late binding.

In java all class methods are early bound and statically dispatched while all instance methods are virtual and hence based on the runtime type a dynamic dispatch is made and the method invocation is late bound.

A virtual function/method table, vtable or dispatch table is used to support late/runtime binding, dynamic dispatch. Vtable is the common implementation used to support dynamic dispatch in languages like C++ and C#.

The compiler typically creates a separate virtual table for each class and in each constructor is puts hidden code to initialize the vtable with the addresses/offsets of the methods. There is also a hidden pointer 'virtual table pointer' for each class.

Lazy Evaluations

Eager evaluation is the opposite of lazy evaluation. The concept is used typically in the context of expression evaluations. Most programming languages have eager evaluation and the expression is evaluated the moment it is bound to a variable. While most functional programming languages follow lazy evaluation, and the expression is evaluated only when there is a need to produce a result which requires the use of the expression.

Delayed evaluation has the advantage of being able to represent list or infinite series of numbers e.g. in F# Fibonacci series can be represented using the lazy expression...

```
let rec fibs = seq {
    yield! [1; 1];
    for (x, y) in Seq.zip fibs (Seq.skip 1 fibs) -> x + y }
```

Now if you want the Nth fibonazzi number only the first N number in the series are enumerated. Problems occur only if programmers carelessly try to count the number of numbers in the infinite series or their sum or a similar operation.

Sequence Expressions/Comprehensions

A sequence expression/comprehension is an expression that evaluates to a sequence (F#). It is different from a list in the sense that evaluation is only done when it is needed.

e.g. seq { 0 .. 10 .. 100 }

creates a sequence from 0 to 100 in steps of 10.

e.g. seq { for i in 1 .. 10 do yield i * i }

the above creates a sequence of squares of 1 to 10.

A sequence expression is a construct in F# that uses lazy evaluation to create sequences. Sequences in F# are like lists. Support operations such as grouping and counting and extraction of sub-sequences.

Monads

Monads are used to structure functional programs. They are a convenient framework for simulating side effects such as global state, exception handling, output, or non-determinism. Pure functional languages like Haskell are pure lambda calculus while impure languages like F# support assignments, exceptions and continuations. Monads are used to integrate impure effects into pure functional languages.

In a pure functional program without any side effects the data flow is very explicit. In such cases how do we carry forward e.g. exception information, stack traces, state and such. In F# monads are also called as computation expressions, which are a generalization of sequence expressions, aka workflows.

Immutable DataTypes

Unfortunately there is no easy mechanism in imperative languages like C# and Java to make data types immutable. By immutable data types we mean that once the data type is created and initialized it is then onwards immutable. This is very important from the point of concurrency and scalability. As concurrent activities don't need to lock or synchronize between them. Input data never changes and in line with functional programming concepts new data is just created.

This results in simpler code. Some architects argue that classes should also be immutable once instantiated, though it seems an infeasible design to implement in all scenarios.

Synchronization

Synchronization of threads is a mechanism whereby marked areas of code can have only one thread accessing them at a time. The region of code is monitored by a monitor object which queues threads and provides access one at a time.

e.g. in C#

```
private System.Object lockThis = new System.Object();
public void Function()
{
   lock (lockThis)
   {
      // Access thread-sensitive resources.
   }
}
```

Such locks are usually reentrant which means in the following situation where another method is called with a lock on the same monitor object the same thread is instantaneously provided access. Without this feature threads would self dead lock more often.

e.g.

```
private Object lock1 = new Object();
public void inc1() {
   synchronized(lock1) {
      // Access thread-sensitive resources.
               printit();
   }
}
public void printit(){
        synchronized(lock1) {
                System.out.println("Printed inside a reentrant locked region");
        }
}
```

C# uses ManualResetEvent, AutoResetEvent, WaitOne and WaitAny mechanisms in producer consumer kind of scenarios apart from the above mechanism.

Native/Green Threads

Green threads are those threads that are scheduled by the Virtual Machine, they were designed so that the VM could provide an appearance of parallel execution on systems that do not have native thread support. Native threads are those threads that are managed by the operating system. Green threads usually run on only one processor and don't distribute load across multiple processors.

Typically green threads perform better on thread activation and synchronization. While native threads perform better on utilizing multi-core systems with better pre-emptive context switching at any time, and waiting for I/O. Green thread processing can switch to another thread only if the running thread explicitly goes into a wait state or yields control. If green threads perform blocking I/O operation it blocks all other threads, which is not the case with native threads, the former should use asynchronous operations to avoid problems.

Native threads run in kernel space while green threads run in user space. A native thread takes up its own entry in the process table and since that is limited it can hit configured limits or run out of system resources.

Delegates/Method/Function Pointers

In C++ passing a reference to a method is called a method pointer in C# the same concept is called a delegate. A delegate declaration is basically a signature to which methods which are attached to it have to comply. A delegate instance is an instantiation of the delegate which points to one method which complies with the delegate contract. The delegate instance can then be invoked.

```
public void mymethod(string a, int b){...}
...
public delegate void Mydelegate(string a, int b);
Mydelegate del = new MyDelegate(mymethod);
del("Hi",3); // del can be passed around like any other object instance
```

MultiCast Delegates/Events

A delegate with a void return type can be added to a event and when the event is fired all delegates are invoked. This is the implementation in C#.

```
public void mymethod(string a, int b){…}
public void mymethod2(string a, int b){…}
…
public delegate void Mydelegate(string a, int b);

public event Mydelegate MyEvent
…
MyEvent+= Mydelegate(mymethod1);
MyEvent+= Mydelegate(mymethod2);
…
MyEvent("Hi",1);//calls both the methods mymethod1 and mymethod2 in the order.
```

Note: Seems to be a very useful compiler candy.

Functors

A function object, functor, functional, functionoid and a function pointer are used synonymously and are refered to any object that can be called like a function.

Java doesn't have first class functions and a functor is expressed by an interface with one method which is usually implemented as an anonymous inner class. In C# functors are implemented as delegates.

In C++ there are two concepts one is the simple pointer to a function and the other is a class which overloads the operator() method and is used as a function object which can be inlined and has a slight performance improvement while a function pointer/delegate carries the context and is heavy but has other uses.

www.ingramcontent.com/pod-product-compliance
Lightning Source LLC
Chambersburg PA
CBHW060454060326
40689CB00020B/4524